A Mother's Love

The unfamiliar

warning signs

of mental illness.

Karleen Ross

A Mother's Love

tellwell

Tellwell Talent
www.tellwell.ca

ISBN
978-0-2288-0870-1 (Paperback)

Dedication

For my second-born. As we walk through darkness, we find our way to the light. Surrendering is never an option. You have taught me that deep inner strength, when surfaced, can conquer any obstacle and set us back on the right path.

To my late mother-in-law. You accepted me with open arms from the moment we first met. You've helped to shape the woman I've become. There were many times I turned to you for conversations about my own struggles and the uncertainty I felt at times with parenting. You were always there with words of wisdom.

Your love and dedication for your family has taught us profound loyalty and to always have each other's backs. You lived a hard life and encountered pain so deep but still found the strength to continue on. Thank you for leaving us with a legacy of love, acceptance without judgment, and family first. Forever in our hearts.

Acknowledgments

To my husband, daughter, three sons, and BFF, thank you for supporting my idea of putting my thoughts to paper in writing this book. You are always a positive voice. Your support means everything.

Introduction

A married mother of four consumed with work and raising a young family begins to see signs of unfamiliar behaviour in her second son.

Unaware of the journey she is about to embark, she realizes that parenting is the most difficult job she will ever experience as she is exposed to something she knows nothing about — mental illness.

Through love, frustration, tears, and learning, she becomes his biggest advocate.

A genuine and heartfelt perspective of a mother caring for a child with mental illness, through various stages and situations of his life.

An emotional but rewarding journey that creates awareness for parents and caregivers, offers hope, and extends support.

Chapter 1

It was April 1994. My then boyfriend (now husband) and I decided that we would try for our second child. We were already new parents to a six-month-old baby boy and my boyfriend's ten-year-older daughter from a previous relationship. Though our first son wasn't planned, he was a beautiful blessing. We didn't want to wait too long between children, as he had done with his daughter.

I was the tender age of twenty-three and he was thirty-three. A full ten years my senior. He was a great guy and had all the characteristics needed to meet my standards of a good husband and father to my kids. I was sure this was what I wanted.

At the age of thirteen, I was diagnosed with scoliosis, a severe curvature of the spine that measured sixty-two degrees by the time I underwent major surgery at the age of fourteen.

After my follow-up appointments which continued for four years, I was always told never to have children. The doctors never really explained why; instead, they just made it sound as though I wouldn't be able to easily conceive. So, when I got pregnant with my first son without even trying, I figured everything was as it should be.

I still wanted to check with my doctor, however, just to make sure my spine was still in good condition and confirm that nothing had shifted during the pregnancy and delivery of my first son.

My appointment day came and I explained to my gynecologist that we were excited to become pregnant again and wanted to start trying right away. After a full review, he gave us the go-ahead to begin trying.

In July, I was told we were six weeks pregnant!

The moment I knew I had another beautiful baby growing inside of me, I was elated!

I was excited and nervous all at the same time, just thinking how full my hands would be with two little ones to manage at once. But as the weeks progressed, I became more excited and less nervous.

When my pregnancy reached eighteen weeks, I had a routine check-up scheduled. I left my son with his babysitter and headed off to my appointment. I mentioned to the doctor that I was feeling a little pressure in my uterus at certain times on and off throughout my day. He asked me to get undressed, slip into a gown, and lay on the bed so he could do an internal examination.

He slowly inserted two fingers and very quickly looked perplexed. He asked me to lay still as he conducted the same exam a second time. He then asked that I sit up and get dressed. He pulled the plastic gloves off, threw them into the trash can, and said he would meet me across the room in his office.

I immediately knew something was wrong.

My face flushed as my eyes widened like a deer caught in headlights. I gently nodded and did exactly what he asked.

As I got dressed, my mind started racing with chaotic thoughts. Thoughts of nothing positive, of course, but not a concrete negative either.

I walked my way over to his desk where he sat waiting for me. As I sat down, he cleared his throat and softly started to speak.

"You are eighteen weeks pregnant and already one-and-a-half centimetres dilated. This is not good. There is a high probability that you are going to lose this baby."

Lose my baby? "Is this man crazy?!" I thought to myself.

"What do you mean, lose my baby?" I repeated in an awkward, high-pitched tone. "No. I'm not!" I insisted.

"You cannot be dilated at such an early stage in your pregnancy. You are at an extremely high risk of miscarriage," he said calmly.

"Ok, so what are we going to do about it then?" I asked in a sharp tone. I suddenly felt the warm tears rolling down my face.

He was an elder doctor, by my guess, well into his sixties, but one of the best doctors in the city and highly recommended. I'm not sure if he realized I had such a sharp tongue. He had taken care of me during my first pregnancy and had only ever seen a young, sweet, pleasant girl, scared but excited. He had put me on bed rest at thirty-one weeks with my first son because, like now, I had become dilated too soon. My first son had arrived unannounced at thirty-six weeks, healthy and simply perfect. But now he was telling me that this pregnancy was not likely going to continue, and I wasn't having any part of accepting this foreseen outcome.

He explained that I would be immediately placed on bed rest. I wasn't to lift anything heavy, stand on my feet too long, walk too far, or have any sex. Well, this was going to be challenge! I had a nine-month-old baby at home.

How the hell was I going to do that? The not having sex part was the least of my worries. I needed to do whatever it took to keep this baby healthy and inside of me.

He told me that if all went well, when my pregnancy reached twenty-four weeks, he would approve me for surgery where he would stich my cervix to help keep the baby secure. He was also prescribing me a drug called Yutopar. This was believed to help delay dilation and premature deliveries.

I was devastated, but at the same time hopeful and extremely determined.

When I arrived home that afternoon, I had to pull myself together several times. The tears just wouldn't stop. I waited for my husband to come home from work, and then I broke down again as I told him our grim diagnosis. He was great. He reassured me that we were in this together and felt that everything would work out.

The next few weeks I did my very best to follow the doctor's orders. The heaviest weight I carried was my young son, who always wanted Mommy. I was happy to oblige.

At twenty-four weeks, I was admitted to the hospital to have the procedure done. It was successful. I stayed in hospital for four days while my mother-in-law took care of my young son.

I was ordered to remain on bed rest for the remainder of my pregnancy. As the weeks continued to roll by, the baby became heavier and heavier. My contractions now occurred daily, and they were always sporadic. I would bleed lightly at random times and always experience low-level abdominal cramping. I was constantly anxious but so happy as each week passed, taking us a little closer to the due date.

At six-and-a-half months, we found out the baby's sex. We were having another boy!

My husband was ecstatic! We talked about the names we liked and had a short list of our top preferences. A few weeks later, I put the task in my husband's hand. He decided. And we affectionately named him Jamal.

Chapter 2

The pregnancy was going as well as to be expected. I continued to follow doctor's orders as best as I could. I would rub my belly constantly and talk to my baby boy, calling him by name each time. He was active and growing nicely. He seemed to get doubly excited at bedtime when I curled up next to my husband. I would lay behind him in a spooning position, and Jamal would kick and float around with excitement. Every time Daddy was around and spoke to him, he seemed to react. It was the sweetest thing.

My due date was supposed to be February 19th, 1995. But we all knew that we would never make it to that date. As well, my doctor had to schedule another surgery in order to remove the sutures from my cervix. I couldn't just allow my body to go naturally into labour, otherwise there would be serious damage done to my inside parts. So, my doctor and I agreed that I would be induced at thirty-six weeks. He felt that was the longest we could wait without causing potential complications. At thirty-three weeks, I began feeling more pressure and the doctor mentioned that Jamal had dropped and was head-down into the birth canal. I was to rest even more, and stay off my feet as much as possible.

My doctor set my induction date for three weeks later, the last week of January (the 27th I believe). But I was insistent that I wanted a February baby! And so, he agreed to induce me on January 31st at 10 p.m. and hope for the best.

I rolled into surgery on the 31st and underwent a twenty-minute procedure to remove the sutures. Next, I was connected to an intravenous with some type of medicine that would start the labor process. It seemed that within a few short moments, I began feeling the familiar pain and discomfort I had felt fifteen months prior with the swift delivery of my first son.

As my husband sat with me, he provided and endured comic relief, hand squeezing, ice chips, vomit bowls, and a few curse words. Four hours later, I was fully dilated, and the nurse paged the doctor who was swift to appear.

With a couple of good, focused pushes and unbelievable sweat, my beautiful baby boy was born at 2:12 a.m. on February 1st, 1995!

He weighed six pounds, ten ounces; had a full head of soft, beautiful black hair; and was simply perfect! He cried only for a moment.

After the nurses cleaned him up and swaddled him tightly in a warm blanket, he was handed to me. I held him to my bosom and stared down into his little face.

"Oh my gosh!" I squealed. "He looks just like you!" I said to my husband. My heart was full.

"We made it, Jamal," I whispered to him softly. "We made it!"

As I looked down at his little face, I knew in my heart this little guy was a fighter.

CHAPTER 3

Jamal was a welcome addition to the family. He was the youngest of three. His sister, now eleven, was already used to playing the role of big sister and helping out with both him and his little-big brother.

Jamal was a calm baby. He only cried when he was hungry or if his tummy was unsettled.

But after a few weeks, I found him to be restless after feeding times. He would spit up the milk he drank and be fussy. As the weeks past, I became more concerned. One day after a feeding, I changed his diaper and was shocked to see there was blood in his stool. I was so freaked out that I immediately packed him up and took him straight to the hospital. He was barely five weeks old.

After being checked by the doctor, they ran a few tests and then advised me that he had an allergy to the milk-based formula I was feeding him. As a result, he had developed an infection causing inflammation in his intestine. They needed to admit him in order to treat it, as it could cause complications if it wasn't treated right away. I was devastated.

We'd already gone through so much to carry him safely to term, and now we had to deal with this diagnosis. I blamed myself for choosing to bottle-feed as I had done with my first son, thinking there would be no issue. But clearly, it wasn't the best choice for him. I quickly snapped out of the blame game and switched my focus to helping my baby get healthy and back home as soon as possible.

Jamal ended up staying in the hospital for five days. I was there all day and night with visits from my husband and my other baby boy. It was a tough stint. But I wasn't going anywhere.

Finally, on the fifth day, he received a clean bill of health with a new all-natural non-milk-based formula that would replace what he was being given. It was called Nutramigen and was ridiculously expensive but regardless the cost, he was going to get it. I took my son home, excited to return to normalcy.

Chapter 4

As Jamal grew and became mobile, we quickly realized that he was a curious and rambunctious little boy. He was nothing like his older brother who was very shy, quiet, and reserved. When Jamal was awake, it was constant running through our apartment, crashing monster trucks together, and bouncing up and down. He was an abundance of energy and always laughter. When he was fifteen months old, he was at home with the babysitter who called me at work in a panic. While bouncing on the couch, Jamal had fallen off and cracked the back of his head open. She said he would need to be taken to the hospital because she couldn't control the bleeding.

I rushed to meet them at the hospital. That night, he received four stitches to his scalp.

We realized that Jamal would influence his older brother to join him in getting into things. They both knew better, but for some reason, Jamal seemed to have the talent of persuading his brother down to an art.

I remember when they were two and three years old, and I put them to bed for an afternoon nap. About thirty minutes later, I heard giggles coming from their shared bedroom. I opened the door to see both holding hands, standing across from each other, and pulling each other back and forth on the hardwood floor that was completely covered with baby lotion!

"OMG! What are you two doing?!" I shrieked. They both froze in place, staring at me like two baby fawns in headlights. They looked at each other with eyes wide open. And before his brother could even articulate a response, Jamal said,

"Not me, Mommy. He did it first!" All I could do was clean them up, command them back to bed, secretly smile, and shake my head.

The boys were three and four when we were blessed again with another pregnancy, this time of our third son. By this pregnancy, I knew exactly what to expect. As a precaution, my doctor once again ordered me to be on bed rest. I was dilated half a centimetre at twenty weeks. Again, he scheduled for me to have the same surgery to suture my uterus at twenty-four weeks to ensure the baby stayed inside for as long as possible.

I was much less stressed about my third pregnancy and knew what I needed to do. Everything happened as it should and at thirty-six weeks, I was induced immediately after having the procedure to remove the sutures.

I was in labour for a whole four hours before the delivery of my beautiful third baby boy!

Having three boys and a daughter now meant we needed a bigger home.

I wasn't happy with the neighbourhood we were living in as there was always some kind of crazy crime or drama happening. It was an area known for drugs and gang-instigated crimes. And every year, it seemed to get worse.

I had been raised in this kind of environment after moving to Canada to be reunited with my mother at the age of six. I was used to seeing things a little kid should never have to see. Because of my environment, I gained street smarts quickly. But that was my childhood. I knew that I wanted better for my children, so I wasn't having any part of raising my children in that same environment. It was time to move on.

We began looking at homes in several neighbouring cities and quickly realized the cost of owning a home was way outside of our budget. If we wanted to own a house, we would need to leave the city completely and look in smaller, rural areas. We decided to look north, about an hour away. I wasn't familiar with the small-town vibe, but the prices couldn't be beat and it seemed like a great place to raise a family. So, with both excitement and uncertainty we bought our first home and decided to commute back to the city every day for work.

It was a sacrifice we were willing to make for the sake of raising our children in a healthy environment.

Chapter 5

As Jamal and his big brother got older, we realized that they were two very different personalities. His brother was captivated by *Star Wars*, comic books, and trading cards, while Jamal was always outside running around playing road hockey, riding his bike, or building bicycle jumps with spare wood and nails he had found in his father's workshop in the garage.

He also loved skateboarding and used his bike jumps to test his skateboarding skills.

He would go into his dad's tool box to try to tighten the screws on his skateboard or to repair his own bike chain if Dad wasn't home. He was an active boy and popular with friends.

We always scheduled quiet time for the boys at least one hour before bed, and Jamal always found comfort in building his LEGO pieces. He would lay on his belly in the middle of the family room on the carpet with all the pieces spread out evenly. He spent a lot of time being creative, which was good to see.

When it came to food, he would stick to what he loved. Grilled cheese sandwiches, macaroni and cheese, French toast, chicken fingers, mashed potatoes, and roast beef. He could eat these things every day without tiring.

Not to say he wouldn't eat other foods I cooked, but those were his staple, go-to foods.

At the age of seven Jamal was selected to play on the hockey "Select" team.

He was a great skater. In fact, as the hockey years rolled on, he continued to play at a competitive level. He quickly earned the nickname "Speedy" because he was such a quick skater!

He loved hockey: ice hockey, road hockey, ball hockey. He watched the NHL teams on T.V. and was always keeping an eye on stats. He and his dad bonded heavily over the sport of hockey.

Playing at a competitive level was exciting, costly, and took a lot of commitment from the entire family.

When there were scheduled out-of-town games and tournaments, it was a family affair. While Jamal and the rest of his teammates were practicing and playing games, his older and younger brothers were bonding and hanging out in the arena and hotel rooms with the other players' siblings. Many times, hockey took us away from participating in other family events, but it was worth it, and we were together.

When Jamal was eight, I accepted a job closer to home. We needed a more balanced home life with the kids. Having both myself and my husband work out of town wasn't cutting it for the needs of our family. The commute to the city was a nightmare.

I was getting up at 5 a.m., getting myself dressed, and then rolling my sleepy boys out of bed to get them dressed and down to the kitchen for breakfast. Then I would direct them to the front door to gather their shoes, coats, and backpacks; organize them in single form into the car; and head to the babysitter for 6:30 a.m. Seriously, just thinking about it now makes me tired.

As good as I was at getting this routine down to a science, leaving the boys at 6:30 in the morning and picking them up 6:30 in the evening was too much to deal with. After three years of that, I was done.

I decided to take a pay cut to be closer to home and more available for the kids.

I accepted a job and worked the afternoon shift, 12 p.m. to 8 p.m.

One evening while at work, my supervisor called me over and said I had an urgent phone call and was to call home right away. I rushed over to the phone and called the house.

Jamal answered. He was in an absolute panic. He said, "Mom, Uncle is dead! Uncle's dead!" At first, I was startled and confused.

I said, "What do you mean, dead?"

"He fell off his bike and he's dead!"

"What?!" This couldn't be! I remember asking him, "Where's Daddy?"

"Daddy's gone to the hospital," he said.

"Ok," I said. "Maybe Uncle fell off his motorcycle and hurt himself and had to go to the hospital."

"No, Mommy, no! He's dead!" he insisted. I felt a panic rush over me. I couldn't even think straight. I told him that I was leaving work and would be home right away.

He was my husband's youngest brother. He was twenty-seven years old. He had bought a motorcycle against my husband's advice and received it that very week on the Tuesday. I remember him coming by the house to show it off to the boys. They were so excited!

Jamal adored his uncle and the new bike was right up his alley. He was in absolute awe.

His uncle had promised he would buy a smaller helmet, good enough to fit the boys, and he would be back on the weekend to take them for a little spin around the big circle that made our crescent.

But that weekend never came. His uncle had indeed been killed in a motorcycle accident within three days of having the bike delivered.

His death was devastating and knocked the wind right out of the entire family. It was undoubtedly the worst day of our lives.

It's hard for parents to know how to deal with death. We try to shield our children from pain and suffering at all costs. It's never an easy thing. Do we allow them to say goodbye? Should they go to the funeral, or not go to the funeral? How do we deal with it? How do we know what's best for the children?

Because of the relationship the boys had with their uncle, especially Jamal, we felt it was important for them to attend the funeral service. We dressed them in little suits. They were so handsome and looked like little men. But the occasion was heart-wrenching.

We went through the motions of the funeral and for weeks after, Jamal would still talk about his uncle. There was definitely a loss that he felt. His behaviour didn't seem to change, or at least not enough where I became concerned, except that he became fiercely protective of his young aunt who was now left on her own.

They were high school sweethearts. They had lived together common-law with plans to marry. Jamal had known her since he was three years old and loved her dearly.

He began asking me who would take care of her and if she would get a new boyfriend. I tried my best to reassure him but I don't think he was confident in my answers.

A few months later, his girlfriend dropped off a few bags with some items. She felt that we would want to keep a few of his belongings.

My husband went through the bags and pulled out his T-shirts and a few other items.

Jamal immediately wanted his uncle's snowboard, even though he clearly would not be able to use it for years!

He also took his uncle's favourite bed comforter and immediately put it on his bed. His aunt had framed a photo of Jamal and his uncle wearing their Boston Bruins hockey jerseys. His uncle was always trying to recruit Bruins fans and had bought Jamal the jersey as a gift the year before his passing.

Jamal immediately placed the picture on the shelf above his bed, and that was where it would stay.

Later that year, I remember doing the boys' laundry and pulling out a pair of underwear from the bottom of their hamper. It was Jamal's, and it was wet.

I thought to myself, "Hmm, that's weird. He must have held his pee too long and not made it to the washroom on time. Silly boy." I remember shaking my head, then shrugging it off.

I wasn't concerned. I didn't want to mention it and have him feel embarrassed. "It's no biggie," I thought. Accidents happen.

The following week, I did the boys' laundry again and found the same. This time, there were a few pairs of wet underwear. I put them in the washing machine and called Jamal into the laundry room.

I told him that I had found his wet underwear in his hamper and asked him if he was holding his pee too long. He shrugged and said, "I don't know." I asked him if he was having accidents at school or at home. He said it was mostly at night when he was sleeping, but sometimes at school a little bit and he would have to run to the washroom. He would never full-out wet his bed. He always woke himself up in time to run to the washroom.

Because he was such an active child, I felt that he was drinking too much and holding it for too long. I told him to be mindful about not waiting till the last minute and that he wasn't allowed to drink anything after 7:30 p.m. We would see if that helped. Of course, that arrangement was difficult when he had evening hockey games, but we tried to stick to the plan as best as possible.

The leaking continued, so I booked an appointment with our doctor, who, after examining him, said it was normal and that he would outgrow it. He didn't seem concerned in the least and advised that I should keep on minimizing his fluids in the latter part of the day.

Jamal was almost nine. His accidental wettings continued until he was twelve. Aside from the accidental wetting and occasional sleepwalking episode to the bathroom, I saw nothing that caused me to panic.

Chapter 6

Over a year after his uncle's passing, Jamal's aunt began seriously dating a new guy. She had been seeing him for a few months and wanted us to meet him. There was going to be a family BBQ hosted by her mother and she invited us. Her new beau would be there.

The moment our family met him, we liked him. He seemed like a genuinely nice person and appeared to have her best interests at heart. Jamal and his brothers took a liking to him right away. Shortly after meeting him, I asked the boys if they liked their aunt's new boyfriend. They all said "yes" with no hesitation. But Jamal was quick to elaborate his feelings. "I like him, he's nice," he said with complete assurance.

"Good! I'm glad," I said.

"Do think it would be okay if I called him my Uncle?"

At first, I didn't quite know what to say. I was so surprised he would even think to ask.

It brought tears to my eyes because in that moment, I knew his little heart was hopeful that now his aunt would no longer be alone and would again have someone to take care of her. And not just any guy, but a guy that he fully approved of!

"Well, I'm not sure about that, Jamal. That's something we'll have to ask," I answered carefully.

"Ok," he said. And off he went to play.

Later that week I called his aunt and told her about our little conversation. She was smitten by Jamal's affection for her beau, and before we knew it, all three boys were happily calling him Uncle.

As well, it turned out that our gut instincts were right! A little over a year later, they were engaged. They would later marry.

Chapter 7

At the age of twelve, Jamal had been playing rep hockey for five years. He still enjoyed it.

It was what he knew.

He was used to early morning practices. We would wake up at 5:15 a.m. to get dressed and off to the arena for 6 a.m.

During the week, his dad and I would be there for ninety-five per cent of his games. I always traded shifts at work to accommodate getting to the arena, and other parents on the team helped out.

A few parents that we became friends with were kind enough to drop him off at the arena for us when we needed help. My husband would hustle throughout his work day, skipping breaks and full lunches just so he could leave work a little extra early to get to the arenas, no matter which city his games were in.

I think because his father was so invested in his success and athletic ability, there were times he would get upset with Jamal's lack of effort. He had such a natural talent, but at times he didn't seem to have his head in the game. It was frustrating for me too because I could see his potential. He was obviously good enough to make the rep teams year after year. But at times, it was clear that he was struggling.

During the games that he exhibited fantastic effort, win or lose, his dad was extremely proud and would tell him so. They would talk about the play and the things he did really well.

After the games where he didn't play well or had a clear lack of effort, his dad was also very vocal. He was always sure to explain the areas that he saw a need for improvement. They would go over the plays and Jamal would understand the feedback his dad was trying to offer. Though it was always said from a place of love, it was clear that Jamal hated disappointing himself. Even more, he absolutely hated disappointing his dad. Around this time is when I took notice of Jamal's nail biting habit.

He had made some good friendships in this brotherhood of hockey, and we allowed him to have playdates and sleepovers at times we felt were appropriate. There were so many times Jamal would ask for a sleepover but by 10:00pm, he would call home and ask us to pick him up. He enjoyed going to play but when night time came, and it was close to bedtime, he would want to come home. It became regular behavior.

As far as we knew, we were very actively involved in knowing who he played with and spent time with. The friends he made, both through hockey and school, came from good families. Although most were not as strict in parenting as we were, we felt they had a positive influence and approved of his friendships.

There were, however, a couple of friendships that we later realized were not in his best interests. These friendships were minimized and monitored heavily.

To this day, I still believe that we did the best we could at raising our children with a level of expectation and standard which gave them a healthy foundation and upbringing.

His dad and I were never naive enough to think we had perfect kids, because kids in general will mess up and do things they aren't supposed to. But that's how kids learn.

At fourteen he started high school. The school we sent him to was the same Catholic high school we had chosen for his older brother, who was two grades ahead.

Unlike his brother, Jamal knew a good number of kids the first day of school through friendships in hockey and other connections.

We aren't Catholic, but we chose to send the kids to a faith-based high school because at the time, the other public high school in our school zone had a terrible reputation with drugs, alcohol, and a lot of issues. So even though most of our children's friends from public school were headed to this other high school, we knew our kids would be fine and would quickly form new friendships.

Once in a while, Jamal would ask to go to a "house party". I usually knew the parents, or else I would drop him off and go to the door to introduce myself and get a feel for the situation. When leaving, I always felt that things were under control.

I noticed that around this age, Jamal would become easily agitated. We used to say that if Jamal wasn't happy, then the entire house couldn't be happy. He never shared any reason for being miserable; he just was. But then shortly after, he would seem to be back to normal.

We figured that it was just his hormones and the life of being a teenager.

He was still very active. Now in high school, he was super excited to join the junior football team! I remember him being so excited to try out. It was late August and he had spent the summer staying in mint condition. During summer, ice hockey was over but he would always keep active and do at least one hockey camp. That summer, he decided to play ball hockey. He also started jogging almost daily. He was always outside. He was constantly on his bike, skateboarding, or playing with his friends and older brother in the forest.

That August, he made me take him to the sports store to find him the perfect pair of cleats for football.

He had an eye for the finer things, aka, more expensive brand-name products. But I told him I wouldn't be spending all kinds of cash for cleats until we knew for sure that he had made the team.

Pardon me for doubting this kid… He made the football team without a hitch!

Like they always said, he was "speedy". He was a great runner and had natural talent.

He was so excited and we were super happy for him!

Playing rep hockey and school football took a lot of time and dedication. Both teams had demanding schedules. At the same time, we also expected him to stay on top of his school work.

There really was no time for him to "hang out". He was kept extremely busy.

After his first year of high school, he decided to end his love affair with playing rep hockey.

It had been a challenging year academically. He received all his credits but like his older brother, we had expectations for what we considered acceptable grades. He received a fifty-two per cent in math, so we enrolled him in summer school to retake the course and upgrade. He wasn't pleased, but the topic was not up for negotiation.

He did well that summer and finished math with a seventy-five per cent average.

Chapter 8

It was sophomore year. His new love was football, and he wanted to focus on it, as well as his grades, and of course... girls. He had a more manageable schedule and had made new friends through classes and his football buddies.

Around that time, it became clearly apparent that Jamal was struggling with sleep. There would be nights that he just could not fall asleep and stay asleep. He would wake up in the morning and be absolutely miserable. I couldn't understand it. I tried to get him to relax at evening time. I would draw warm baths for him and add lavender. I would spray his pillow with lavender and make him warm decaffeinated herbal teas.

Nothing seemed to help. I started taking him and his brothers to the library every other week to choose the books they would enjoy reading at rest time. Jamal would always choose good storybooks to read, but he would only manage to get through about half before it was time to return them.

I finally made an appointment and took him to our doctor to see if there was any reasoning behind his insomnia.

He had been the boys' doctor since they were little. When I explained the episodes, he had no real concerns. He said that I should ensure Jamal had minimal light stimulation before bed, which meant not letting him play video games, watch T.V., or play with his cell phone directly before bedtime.

I started giving him melatonin before bed to see if it would help rest his mind. Nothing seemed to work.

It was an ongoing battle with sleep.

I remember him waking up in the morning for school. He would be getting dressed and just sit at the end of his bed in tears.

"I just want to sleep, Mom. Why can't I sleep?" he would say.

It seemed impossible for him to get a proper night's sleep.

I remember feeling so sad for him that I allowed him to stay home once in a while to go back to bed and actually sleep. It was both sad and frustrating as a parent to see him that way and not be able to do anything to fix it.

At fifteen, I noticed that Jamal's posture was off. I immediately took notice because of my history with scoliosis. I'd always been told the gene was much rarer in boys but nonetheless, it was a strong gene and it was hereditary.

One day, as he stood looking in the fridge, I asked him to stand up straight. "I am," he said. I had him lift up his shirt and stand in front of me with his back towards me. I told him to bend forward and touch his toes. As he did that, I ran my fingers down his spine and could feel there was a slight curve. I thought that since I was the only one to see it, maybe I was overreacting, so instead of freaking out, I decided to keep a close eye on it.

About nine months later, my mother came for a visit. I saw her staring at Jamal as he stood in the kitchen. "Jamal, stand up straight," she said.

Again, he said, "I am, Grandma." My mom looked at me, I looked at her, and we both knew. She made me promise to book an appointment and get him to the doctor as soon as possible.

The following month, the doctor booked a specific X-ray for detecting scoliosis. He advised that if Jamal's spine was any more than thirty-two degrees curved, he would be recommended to a pediatric neurosurgeon at the children's hospital in the city. The results came in. His curve measured forty-two degrees.

We waited three months to receive an appointment date, then another six months before we saw the neurosurgeon in the clinic at the children's hospital. During this waiting period, Jamal had a growth spurt which caused his back pain and discomfort to become more consistent.

Our first meeting with the surgeon was July, the summer before his grade eleven year.

The doctor physically assessed Jamal's spine, and then he sent him downstairs for new X-rays to get a current and accurate reading on the degree of the curvature.

The results? In a matter of nine months, his curve had increased from forty-two per cent to sixty per cent.

Wow. It was incredible. Not only was he now experiencing terrible back pain at times, but he was also still playing school football, first string, and he refused to stop.

After reviewing the new X-ray results, the surgeon advised us that Jamal would definitely require surgery. He explained to him that the surgery was very serious and would eliminate him from playing any contact sports such as hockey and football for a minimum of two years, based on how he felt. The surgery would be eight hours long and there was a possibility he may need a blood transfusion due to the amount of blood loss. He also said Jamal would be in the hospital for seven days following the surgery.

Jamal was devastated. He absolutely loved sports and now wouldn't be able to play any of them for a long time.

I remember watching my son as the doctor spoke and feeling so very sad for him.

I could see his body physically react to the news being delivered. But I knew it was not something we could ignore. Surgery had to be done.

He was placed on the surgery list and would have to wait another six months for the operation.

Because his surgery wasn't going to be until January of the following year, Jamal insisted that he play one last season of football for his grade eleven year.

Football ran from the end of August to mid-December (if they made it all the way). Regardless of the pain and discomfort he was in, he made up his mind that he was going to go out with a bang! He played the season and indeed finished on top.

Their team won the championship and it was a great end to his high school football journey!

During the months leading up to the surgery, Jamal was still suffering from lack of peaceful, enjoyable sleep. He also started losing weight and had no appetite. I became worried because he was so active but then so quickly lethargic.

My husband told me that I was just being overly concerned and reminded me that Jamal had always been sporadic with his eating patterns. He would eat three full meals solid for one month, and then for the next couple of months not want to eat at all. He would become really picky.

We chalked it up to picky eating and teenage hormones, though when he was home, all he seemed to want to do was lay in bed.

One night as I lay sleeping, I heard a sound as though someone had slipped on the stairs. I quickly jumped up and opened my bedroom door. Right away I could see that Jamal's bedroom door was wide open. He wasn't in the washroom, so I called out for him and heard nothing.

I walked down to the main floor and could see that the lights to the basement stairs were on, so I walked down into the basement.

When I looked to my left, I could see the light was turned on in the boys' gaming room.

It was a teen den for "men" that my husband had created for our boys and their friends.

I walked into the room to find Jamal sitting on the lounge chair in his boxer shorts, eyes wide open looking up at the blank T.V. screen mounted on the wall.

"Jamal," I said gently. "What are you doing down here?" He didn't answer. I walked up to him and could clearly see that even though his eyes were wide open, he was still very much asleep. I gently took his hand and said, "Ok buddy, let's go back to bed." I helped him stand, and then I took him by his shoulders and shuffled him into the hallway. I positioned my body directly behind him as I moved my hand gently to the middle of his back. He willingly allowed me to guide him back up the stairs and directly into bed. I covered him up and stood in the doorway watching him for a few moments as he closed his eyes and seemed to fall into a deep sleep.

That night, I laid awake for hours. It wasn't until the early morning that I fell into somewhat of a semi-sleep mode. "Another sleepless night", I thought to myself.

The next morning, while he sat eating breakfast, I told him what had happened.

"Ya right, Mom. There's no way." He completely denied it even being possible.

He didn't know any better. But I was concerned. Very concerned.

I asked him if there was anything that was bothering him. He said no. I asked him about school, his girlfriend, and even the upcoming surgery. Everything he said was fine. But he did have a lot of questions for me about how he would feel after the operation.

He wanted to hear from someone who had gone through it, and that was me.

I tried to be very honest with him about what to expect and I remember him saying to me with sarcasm, "Thanks a lot, Mom."

I asked him, "For what?"

He replied, "For giving me these crappy scoliosis genes." At the time I didn't really take it too personally. I felt he was just being dramatic and was generally frustrated with the fact that he had to deal with this. In my mind, I felt that he should be at ease in seeing that my surgery had gone well. After all this time, I was still perfectly fine and was leading a very productive life. I felt that he should have seen that even though there were certain sports and things I couldn't physically do, regardless, my life was good!

What I didn't see or realize at the time was that my son was hiding a real problem. He was hiding feelings of severe anxiety. Being as active as he was while knowing it would all come to an end very soon must have been so hard for him to accept.

He continued showing signs of anxiety up to the date of his surgery. He had a few more sleepwalking episodes as well but we dismissed it as him being overtired because he was experiencing such bad insomnia. He still had occasional days where he was so tired, there was nothing he could do but break down and cry.

We didn't realize there was so much more going on inside of him.

CHAPTER 9

Jamal was now seventeen. His girlfriend at that time seemed to be a real sweetheart and appeared to have everything together. They were together over a year. But as time passed, we realized that she was dealing with her own emotional difficulties and issues within her family.

I became concerned one night when Jamal called me after 11 p.m. in a panic.

He was supposed to sleeping at a friend's who lived around the corner from his girlfriend's father's house. But when he called me, he was upset about something going on at **her** house. He didn't know what to do and needed my help.

I quickly jumped in the car and drove over to see what was going on.

When I pulled up to the house, I saw Jamal standing on the driveway waiting for me. He was visibly upset. I didn't know what to think and instantly felt a rush of panic. "What's wrong?" I asked, jumping out of the car.

"She freaking out! I don't know what to do," he said.

"Why? What happened?" I asked. He couldn't explain.

"She's in the house. She's threatening to kill herself because she's so unhappy."

"What?!" I gasped in disbelief. I didn't even know what to say. I immediately asked Jamal if *he* was ok.

He nodded through his tears and said "Yes."

I told him to stay on the driveway and wait for me to talk to her. He agreed.

As I slowly walked into the house through the wide-open front door, the house seemed empty. I called out to her. There was no answer. But I knew where to go because all I could hear was a young girl sobbing. She was sobbing with such intensity, as if her entire world had just been ripped right out from under her.

I followed the crying and stood in the doorway of a bedroom filled with clothes thrown everywhere from the bed, to the ground, to the dresser tops, and over the door. There were posters of cute boy bands plastered on every wall. And in the middle of all the girlie decorative chaos, sitting in the centre of the bed, was a teenaged girl sobbing so hard she could barely breathe. I rushed over to her and gently pulled her into my arms. "Honey, what's wrong? What happened?" She began to cry even harder. It took a few minutes before I could settle her down enough to talk to me.

We talked for a good while about what she was feeling and why. She explained her distress with a difficult relationship she was having with her mother and the lack of attention she felt from her father.

She was an only child between divorced parents and was dealing with so many emotions. She felt that she had no one to talk to and was battling severe depression and anxiety on her own. And on this particular night, she had become overwhelmed with emotion. Unfortunately, it had unleashed itself in Jamal's presence.

I comforted her and told her how special and important she was and even though she may not have felt it, there were so many people who loved and cared about her.

I shared with her my own personal story of pain and recovery and how happiness is possible, even when it may seem so incredibly impossible.

She seemed to be very moved by my story and almost seemed to have an "ah-ha" moment of realization. She became visibly calmer and I was glad for it.

After talking more and bringing her to a calmer level, I told her that I needed to call her mother and that I was willing to drive her there to spend the night. But she begged me not to. She insisted that if her mom knew about this "meltdown" episode, she would have her committed, as she had apparently threatened to do in the past.

It was hard for me to believe, but telling her I would talk to her mother made her so upset with panic that I decided to give her two ultimatums.

I told her she needed to have a girlfriend come over and spend the night with her. And she also needed to talk to her mother the following day and have an honest conversation about how she was feeling and ask for the help she so desperately needed.

I told her I would be following up the next day. If she didn't keep her end of the deal, I would have no choice but to have a one-on-one talk with her mom.

She agreed. Jamal and I waited for her friend to show up before we left.

That night I don't think I slept a wink.

I replayed the episode over and over again in my mind. I was so unsettled with the whole thing. As soon as I woke the next morning, I checked with Jamal to see if he had spoken to her yet, and he had. In fact, they had texted each other and talked through most of the night. He said she sounded better and was being picked up by her mom later that day.

I monitored Jamal's behaviour very closely that day and tried to be inconspicuous with my gentle probing questions.

Kids are always very guarded when they are feeling stressed, protective, or anxious, and I was sure that this situation was causing him to feel all the above.

It can be very difficult to get any information from kids about how they are really feeling, so I realized my questions needed to be short but direct.

"Have you talked to her this morning?"

"Yup."

"Did she sound better?"

"Yup."

"Has she talked to her mother yet?"

"Ya, she's picking her up later to spend the night with her."

"Ok, great! Was this the first time this happened, or has it happened before?"

"Ya, it has, but not like this. She has depression and takes medicine. Sometimes she loses it, but not like last night."

I was shocked, but I tried not to show any emotion.

"Oh, okay. How did you feel when it was happening? Were you scared?"

"Ya, of course. She was freaking out, Mom! I didn't even know what to do!" he replied.

We had a good discussion about the incident and decided that we would let her parents handle it. Jamal needed to offer his support while trying not to become consumed with her problems. I tried to let him know that it was okay to feel confused about what had happened, but also understand how important it was to talk about his feelings and deal with any unsettled emotions. As most teens do, he dismissed the idea of getting into any real details and shrugged it off, saying, "Ya, she'll be alright. I'm good."

I decided to leave things as they were and not reach out to her mother.

I started replaying Jamal's words in my head: "She has depression and takes medicine."

What? Why? She was sixteen. What on Earth? I was so surprised to hear those words, and I didn't know how to feel about it. And to be honest, I didn't know enough about it to have an honest opinion. All I knew was that she needed help and I didn't want my son to be impacted. This was new. It was unsettling.

Chapter 10

A couple of months after the episode, Jamal's surgery date arrived. His eighteenth birthday would be the following month. He seemed anxious to just get the surgery over and done with.

We arrived at the hospital at 6 a.m., and he was prepped and greeted by the OR team of doctors. The surgery would take eight hours. We hugged him and assured him that things would be ok. We would see him soon.

Because I had gone through the same surgery as a teen, I knew exactly what to expect. I felt I was the perfect example of how "Ok" would really look like after such a serious operation. After Jamal was rolled in for surgery, his father and I decided we would go shopping for a new vehicle. After all, we had eight hours to kill.

We left our cell phone numbers with the nurses to call us with any updates if needed and assured them we would be in close proximity and could get back to the hospital quickly.

We spent the day shopping and arrived back at the hospital around the six-and-a-half-hour mark.

Soon after, I received a call on my cell phone that Jamal was out of surgery and things had gone very well! We would have to wait an hour to see him, but everything had gone according to plan and the doctor was pleased.

We waited to be called into the recovery area and with excitement dashed in to see our boy.

When we walked in, Jamal was awake and laying on his side. He gave us a weak smile. I kissed his forehead and asked him how he was feeling.

"Okay," he said sleepily.

"Everything went good!" my husband said, gently patting his head. "You're going to be just fine."

Jamal was a trooper! He was adamant that he would heal quickly and be able to do things again on his own without assistance, so much so, that when we returned to the hospital the next day for a visit, the nurse shared that he had persuaded her to help him roll out of bed, sit up, stand, and take his first few steps towards the door! She was so impressed because typically it was not until the day after surgery when they would have the patient attempt to do this.

Mentally, he was determined to get back to physical normalcy as soon as possible.

Physically, because of his many years of playing rep hockey and football, he was very well-conditioned to push himself. His progress and determination exceeded his surgeon's expectations. In fact, instead of staying in the hospital for the seven days that were scheduled, he was discharged on the fifth day.

As the months rolled on, Jamal continued to do very well. During this time, he and his girlfriend broke up. Ultimately, I think it was his decision to end the relationship. Even though the breakup seemed to be painful for him, I think he realized the relationship just wasn't working out and no longer made either of them happy.

It was a mature thing to do, and silently, I was happy he'd done it.

Jamal continued to do well physically. He was happy with his progress but extremely unhappy that he could no longer play sports anytime soon. He could definitely not play any impact sports, which were all he'd ever played with hockey and football. The more physically fit he felt, the harder it became for him to accept that he was still unable to engage in the sports he loved.

We noticed during this time that he would become very irritable much more easily than normal, and we asked, "What's wrong with you? Why are you so crusty?"

He would respond with an even more irritable response: "Nothing." And off to his room he would go. We honestly felt that it was partly being a teen, partly him missing being active, as well as this just being a part of his personality.

It was hard to decipher. And to be honest, most of the time he acted this way, I myself was very annoyed. I used to say to him, "Just because you are in a crappy mood doesn't mean the rest of us deserve to be in a crappy mood. But when you aren't happy — then everybody else has to be unhappy because you're so miserable."

Looking back, I'm actually non-apologetic for the types of comments I would make, for the simple fact that they were true. I had a house full of other people in it. It wasn't like Jamal was an only child. I had his older brother, younger brother, grandpa, my husband, and a twenty-something-year-old stepdaughter who frequently visited. With a full house and lots of personalities to deal with, focusing all my time and energy on one child and his "poor attitude" was just simply frustrating for me.

CHAPTER 11

Jamal was never rude or unmannerly. That was never the problem. We had always raised our children with a firm but loving hand. Disrespect in the home was simply not tolerated, and to be honest, it was almost never exercised or tested by them.

We'd always had a very good relationship with our kids and they openly shared a lot of things with us. And for that, we were truly thankful.

But unbeknown to his dad and I, Jamal didn't feel that he could openly talk to either of us about his true feelings and what he was actually going through. And I don't believe that he himself understood his feelings either. Whatever he was feeling, he didn't trust us enough to share it.

Our home was a house full of testosterone. There was always fun being poked at one another and competitions of male dominance. There was no room for "babies". So, when Mama Bear babied any of her cubs, eyes would roll and wide grins would poke lighthearted fun.

As the year rolled on, Jamal's "attitude" became normalcy for the family.

One minute he was fine and happy-go-lucky, and the next minute he would be quiet, easily irritated, and genuinely unhappy. We couldn't figure him out, and to be honest, we simply stopped trying to. The ironic thing was, Jamal was such a funny kid. He would say the funniest things that would crack us up. So when he was the Jamal we knew, he was great!

It was those "off" moments that not only frustrated me but left me confused.

He graduated high school the following year at eighteen and started dating a very sweet girl named Carrie whom he genuinely adored. She was upbeat, very personable, and adored him just as much. I remember him saying, "Yup, I think she's the one, Mom." At the time, my husband and I would look at each other and smile, thinking, "You are way too young to know." But at the same time, we both felt completely content with the idea.

Jamal had always talked about joining the army. Carrie was from a military family and he was even more excited by the idea that she was contemplating becoming a military nurse.

He began studying to take the military recruitment test.

Excited, he set the date.

On the day of the test, I wished him luck and told him to make sure he texted me to let me know how things went.

His text never came. And when it did come later that day, it simply read, "I failed."

When I arrived home from work, I sat with him and talked about the test. It seemed he wasn't as upset as he had been earlier in the day as he had talked to the recruitment officer who assured him that it was not an easy test to pass. Apparently, many people from all walks of life and career backgrounds were not successful the first time around.

He seemed hopeful that later in the year, he would make another attempt.

Jamal and Carrie had been dating for about a year when one day he called me upstairs into his room. He said he wanted to talk to me. I remember stepping inside his room and closing the door while looking into his face.

He held his head down and shifted his weight from one foot to the other. I could tell he was uneasy about whatever it was he wanted to talk about.

My tone was low but clear. "What's wrong? What happened?" He began his story by saying, "I didn't want to say anything, but Carrie thinks I should talk to you guys."

"Okay, about what?" I asked.

"Well," he said uneasily, "I don't really know what's wrong with me. I just know I'm not happy."

"Okay," I said. "Well, it's normal to not feel happy sometimes."

"No Mom," he said, his voice expressive. "It's not sometimes; it's all the time. I don't know... I can't explain it. Sometimes I feel fine, then it just switches again and I don't."

"Okay," I said. I started to get a little concerned. "Are you stressed out about something? How are things with you and Carrie?"

"No, it's not that. We're good. It's just me. I barely sleep; I don't eat because I don't feel like eating hardly. I don't know what's wrong with me."

"Jamal, I know that being a teenager is hard. There are a lot of emotions that you feel, and sometimes you don't really know why you have them. But..."

"Mom, I tried to kill myself," he said. "I took a handful of pills and went to sleep. I didn't want to be here anymore."

I felt my eyes widen and immediately swell with tears, my ears became warm, and my heart literally pause for two seconds. Or so it felt.

Those words stopped me dead in my tracks.

"What?! What do you mean?" I shrieked in complete disbelief. "When? Why? Why would you do that?"

"I slept at my friend's house that night and just didn't want to be here anymore. I didn't want to feel like this anymore. So I took a handful of pills and went to sleep. I wasn't expecting to wake up. I didn't want to. But I did."

"Oh my God!" I said. As I watched the tears stream down his cheeks, I felt the tears streaming down mine.

I remember grabbing him into my arms and squeezing him, telling him, "Jamal, there is nothing in this world that is bad enough to make you feel like you don't want to be here anymore. There is nothing we can't work through. Promise me that you'll never do that again."

"I'm sorry," he sobbed. "I'm sorry, Mom. I know."

I sat down on his bed still trying to wrap my mind around what he had just confessed. I felt helpless and completely clueless. This wasn't in the parenting rule book... What the hell was I supposed to do with this? How was I supposed to fix this?

In my mind, as parents, if we raise our kids the best we can by allowing them to experience difficulties and sometimes failures, we are teaching them about the real world and that life isn't all rainbows and unicorns. We try to teach them that when you fail, you do what you have to do, to get up and get back on track. Almost any situation they encounter growing up can be fixed, learned from, and then we move on.

But **this**...These were uncharted waters. I had no idea what I was supposed to do to fix it.

But the one thing I **did** know, was that no matter what it took, I would be there to support my son one hundred per cent.

I knew he needed to talk to someone who was professionally qualified. He needed someone who could understand what he was going through and help him.

I sat with him a few more minutes and we talked. I hugged him tight and told him that I loved him. I assured him that we would make sure to get him to talk to someone about his feelings and what he was going through. It seemed like a burden had been lifted off his shoulders. I noticed an almost immediate relief in him physically.

But for me — my reality had just been flipped on its head.

That night, I didn't sleep a wink.

Chapter 12

I spent the next few days constantly talking to Jamal about how he was feeling and closely monitoring his actions. I contacted the employee assistance program through my work which offered resources for crisis lines and counselling.

Jamal was assigned a counsellor right away to discuss his feelings. He was booked to meet with this counsellor four days after telling me about his situation.

Waiting for his first counselling meeting caused me severe anxiety.

I was constantly worried about him. What was he thinking? How was he feeling? How was he sleeping? I was a ball of nerves, overanalyzing his movements and everything he said and did. I was driving myself crazy and needed my own support system.

The first person I called after Jamal told me about his attempted suicide was my best friend. We had been best friends since we were seventeen.

She was my rock, my ride-or-die chick. A BFF that knew me better than anyone and who knew and loved Jamal and his brothers like her own.

I called her as I sat on the couch with a hot cup of tea and a warm blanket wrapped around my legs. As I explained to her everything that Jamal had shared with me, I broke down and cried. I was honestly scared. I didn't know what to say or what I needed to do to fix it.

I knew there were people who could talk to him and get inside his head better than I could. But I wasn't sure that would even be enough.

Talking to her felt good. I was able to talk out my own feelings because by doing that, I was in a sense counselling myself and being counselled. It was genuinely therapeutic for me.

By the time my husband came home from work later that night, I was in a better head space to calmly explain to him my conversation with Jamal and discuss how we would proceed.

First, I should explain that my husband is very old-school. He was raised in the Caribbean by a single mom and a firm hand. He was already conditioned to a difficult upbringing and felt that nowadays, most kids in general were being coddled by their parents and had no coping skills for disappointments and challenges in life.

There were many times during our own relationship where he felt I was guilty of doing the same with our kids.

There were times when we would both have to take a step back and think about the best (unified) way we needed to discipline or reward our children.

This is not to dismiss the fact that I, too, am old-school in many ways.

Also from the Caribbean and raised by a strong single mother, I felt that I wanted my children to be raised with the same values of respect and kindness. But they also needed to feel loved and supported and have a voice.

Growing up, I couldn't have an opinion when I was being punished or wrongfully accused of something I didn't do. Having an opinion and voicing it was deemed as being rude and talking back.

When I was punished, I wasn't allowed to speak my peace. I took orders and couldn't question them. It wasn't that kind of home.

I didn't want that for my kids. We allowed our children to have a voice, as long as it was in a respectful way, meaning using respectful tone and language.

We were all for it. Allowing them to have a voice when they were in trouble didn't mean they could talk their way out of punishment. But it did allow them to express themselves and their thought processes. Sometimes they would come to their own realization that what they did or said may not have been the smartest thing.

So, with our history of upbringing in mind, my husband had a hard time believing that Jamal was struggling with "depression".

He was upset to know that his son had tried to take his own life, but he refused to call it depression. In his mind, the word "depression" was being thrown around and everyone that felt "sad" was being labelled as "depressed".

In his mind, that simply wasn't his son.

He felt Jamal was going through tough teen years and felt he had anxiety about the direction he wanted to take in college. He felt he'd been disappointed by not passing the military test, by not being able play the sports he loved anymore, and by feeling confused about his career path. To my husband, **that** was the diagnosis.

And looking back, by all accounts, he was partially right.

Jamal **was** upset about all those things. However, in my mind, it was one thing for my son to feel disappointed and confused about some crappy events and circumstances that happened in his young life, but it was a completely different thing to know that the pain he was feeling was so deep and so real that he no longer wanted to live.

That wasn't disappointment. That was depression at the lowest point in his life.

It was darkness that was so real, he tried to do something severe to delete it — forever.

Both of us, to some extent, agreed to disagree.

The only people who were aware of Jamal's depression was my mother, my mother-in-law, and my two best friends. To some extent, it was talked about with our other children but nothing in detail. It was something kept very private.

When I dropped Jamal off at his first counselling appointment, I encouraged him to be open and honest with his feelings. I assured him the counsellor was not there to judge him but instead to help him put his feelings into perspective and help to teach him proper coping skills.

He seemed nervous, but that was to be expected.

An hour later when I pulled up to pick him up from the appointment, he was waiting for me outside and hopped in the car quietly.

I waited a minute before asking him how things went.

"Fine," he said.

I tried asking him if he felt any better after having the conversation.

He shrugged and said, "Not really."

"Ok," I said. "Maybe the next appointment will be better."

He said nothing and sat quietly as I drove home.

Weeks passed and Jamal continued to be the same.

He was moody. He stayed in his room and didn't have much of an appetite. He was happy one day and miserable the next.

I never asked him direct questions about his feelings because I would never get a straight and honest answer. As well, I left him to discuss those feelings with the counsellor.

His second appointment was scheduled with the same counsellor.

This time I left him the car to drive himself. When he picked me up from work, he seemed sombre and quiet.

I purposely waited a little while before asking, "How did things go today at your appointment?"

"I'm not going back," he said in a sharp tone.

"Jamal, you have to give it a chance," I said with a sternness in my voice.

"No Mom, the guy is an idiot! He doesn't talk. He just lets me do all the talking and he just sits there and says nothing. If I wanted to talk to myself, I could just stay home and have a conversation with myself. He's an idiot and I'm not going back!" he insisted.

I was disappointed.

"Alright," I said. If that ***was*** the case, I understood his reasoning. "We'll see about getting you a different counsellor."

Chapter 13

When you feel a connection and you feel heard, it is much easier to be open and accepting of help.

After a few failed attempts, Jamal finally connected really well with his new counsellor, Rhonda.

Once a week he would meet with her. He would come home in a much more pleasant mood and seem less irritated.

I always asked him general questions just to be able to get a feel for how the sessions went and how he was progressing. He never told me specifics, but after his sessions I always had a good indication if it was going to be a good day or a bad day.

I felt that when she asked him to do something outside of his comfort zone, he would be irritated and have anxiety about it. But if it was within his comfort zone, he was fine. It really depended on the conversation and the homework she assigned him each week.

The following year Jamal turned twenty. I was pleased that he had enrolled in his first year of college. He was excited about his course and going back to school.

He had enrolled in Social Work.

He felt he wanted to make a difference by working with youth and young adults dealing with struggles like depression, anxiety, and generally feeling like they didn't fit in because of social awkwardness.

He felt passionate about working with this specific group.

Later that fall I came home to him telling me that he had decided to end things with Carrie.

He said he still cared about her a lot, but he couldn't handle a relationship right now. He needed to be alone and work on himself. He was obviously upset but I commended him for making such a big decision in an attempt to better himself.

Three weeks later, they were back together again. But the following month, they both decided the original break up was best and they parted ways.

As parents, my husband and I always avoided becoming invested in any of our children's romantic relationships. They were young and we knew that relationships would come and go. At the end of the day, our children's happiness was what mattered most. But this breakup, to my surprise, made both of us just a little sad. She was a great girl and we missed seeing her around our house. We missed seeing her and Jamal together. But it had to be done.

Focusing on himself, Jamal reconnected with his friends and started showing some enthusiasm.

He began going out more often, though he was still, by my account, very much a homebody. But he seemed to be doing better.

From what I assumed, he was also doing what his counsellor had suggested by writing out his thoughts and feelings.

I bought him a journal and would often ask him, especially when I could see he was easily agitated or visibly down, "Did you write in your journal this week?"

The answer was often, "Ya."

First semester appeared to be going well.

He seemed very interested in the course, but still I could see his mental health was a daily struggle. By the end of semester one, he started having anxiety about writing his upcoming exams. But he got through them and actually did really well! I was so proud of him and relieved that he had completed the first part of the year.

A few days after writing his final exams, he came home from a counselling session and told me his counsellor had suggested he take a break from school. "Why would she suggest that?" I asked.

"Because I told her I can't deal with it right now. I need a break," he said, clearly frustrated.

"Okay, but why? I thought you were doing better? You just finished your first semester. You wrote your exams and felt you did really well. Why would you delay things now and put school on hold? Just finish the rest of the year and get it over and done with," I said, my tone sharp and unimpressed.

"No, Mom. I'm just not ready," he insisted.

Honestly, I felt myself immediately getting so annoyed at the whole idea of him dropping out.

In my mind, it wasn't a break. It was him dropping out, giving up, and giving in, because it felt too hard.

I wanted to shake him and say, "Get it together! Do you think I feel like getting up every morning and going to work every damn day? Don't you think there are times that I just want to stay in bed, or lay around on the couch watching chick flicks and not doing anything? When I was your age…"

Of course, I wanted to scold him. I hated that he was even thinking this way.

I wanted to give him a reality check! He needed to know that I couldn't just quit when I felt like it. Why? Because I had something called responsibilities and commitments and I couldn't just decide to give up because I felt shitty. Life didn't work that way! And yes — life can be shitty. Real shitty. But guess what? That's just life...

That's what I truly wanted to say.... But something in his eyes made me stop.

As I watched him struggling to find the words to explain why he didn't feel he could go through another semester, his eyes were saying so much more than his mouth.

There was a sadness, a lost and scared look behind his eyes that brought immediate calm to my pissed-off brain.

I took a moment of silence, and then I told him that if he really felt taking a break was necessary, I would be fine with it and would support him.

But I also told him not to make a rash decision in the moment and to sleep on it.

The deadline to pay full tuition for second semester was approaching and I needed to know where things stood.

He agreed to sleep on it and let me know.

The following week, Jamal decided that yes, he would proceed with second semester.

I was happy! But I asked him repeatedly if he was sure.

"Ya, I guess," he said unconvincingly. "I need to get it done."

"Okay," I said. "Great!"

Ten days into semester two, he quit.

Chapter 14

Jamal continued seeing his counsellor.

He would have good days and bad days.

Each day with Jamal, I went through the motions of secretly assessing his mood, behaviour, and overall general attitude. It would take me just a minute to know if he was okay, or struggling.

A few months after the breakup, we had decided to sell our house. We bought a new home not far away and began preparing for our move a few months later in January.

I wasn't too concerned with upsetting the balance of our home because nothing was really changing, except for our address, since we would be living in the same general area. Jamal's younger brother would still be going to the same high school and everyone else would have the same commute to work. Jamal seemed excited about the new home and was looking forward to a change.

On moving day, we had our three boys, Grandpa, myself, my stepdaughter, my best friend and her two sons (who are my godsons), and a handful of Jamal's good friends. Lots of muscle.

Aside from losing an entire shoe rack of the family's shoes and boots that were accidentally tossed out at the city dump, and having to rent a bigger truck last minute, the move went well.

We were blessed to have the help we did and truly appreciated everyone coming together for our family.

Our new home was great but we were short one bedroom, so we made a makeshift bedroom for my youngest son in a cozy part of our unfinished basement.

Within four months, my handyman husband had created two bedrooms and a bathroom in the basement. Jamal decided to relocate to the second bedroom in the basement along with his younger brother. It was their perfect little secluded space where they both settled in nicely.

By now Jamal had celebrated his twenty-first birthday.

He started working again at his previous full-time job.

Again, his moods were up and down.

I started seeing a pattern. He would come straight home, take a shower, and go to bed.

At dinnertime, I was always mindful of what I was cooking and hoped it would encourage his appetite. But more often than not, he wasn't hungry and would skip dinner.

He would drink lots of bottled water throughout the day, but he just didn't have an appetite.

He complained his stomach was constantly cramping and it took nothing for him to have an episode of diarrhea. He had insomnia at night and wouldn't fall asleep until early morning, which made him completely miserable when he had to get up and go to work.

I couldn't figure it out. Within two months, he had lost nearly twenty pounds. Since there was no weight to lose to begin with, because he was already very lean and athletically built, he looked way too thin and borderline unhealthy.

One night as I sat at the table doing some work on my laptop, I decided to research the symptoms of depression.

The information that I saw was as though they had been watching my son and created the characteristics exactly to match his. I was astounded by the similarities.

Everything he was feeling, and all of the behaviours he was displaying, were listed as symptoms of severe depression.

1. Feelings of helplessness
2. Unexplained aches and pains
3. Negative self-talk, self-loathing
4. Loss of energy
5. Easily angry or irritable
6. Appetite or weight changes
7. Sleep pattern changes

I felt sick to my stomach and completely helpless.

The following day, I made an appointment for him to see our family doctor for the upcoming week.

He went to the appointment on his own. When he got home, I asked him how the appointment went. He said the doctor had ordered blood work and would call him with an update if anything was wrong. I could tell he was irritated because nothing was fixed. And I knew deep down all he wanted was to be fixed.

When Jamal's blood work came back, it revealed he was lacking vitamin B12.

The doctor felt that if he increased his B12, he would see a difference in how he felt.

I should point out that even though Jamal was very aware of his depression, he never once wanted or requested medication, and neither did our doctor ever offer any. The doctor felt, as my husband did, that Jamal was simply going through what most young people experience and eventually these feelings would pass.

I think in Jamal's mind, he just wanted to battle his depression in his own way. And from what I could tell, our doctor felt that he was just a young man going through normal emotions that could be combated with the proper coping skills.

I was swift in buying a bottle of B12 and he was diligent in taking it daily.

Nothing seemed to change. After almost a month, he was still constantly sleeping, he had no energy to go out with his friends, he would constantly call in sick to work, or he would show up at work but leave early because he wasn't feeling well. He just seemed genuinely depressed. By this time, he had stopped talking to his counsellor.

She had always been great at motivating him to the extent where I could see a visible difference in his effort. She assured him that she was always just an email away and would make time to see him if and when he wanted to resume his sessions with her. But at this point, he wasn't interested in reaching out to her or anyone else for that matter.

He just seemed so consumed with sadness. I didn't know what I could do to change it, or how I could help fill the void of whatever it was he was feeling.

I talked to him about the possibility of medication. I told him my hope was that he wasn't avoiding discussing it because of the stigma that surrounded mental health and taking medication to help with the effects.

He said he just didn't want to take anything. He just wanted to feel normal and happy, like other "normal" people.

He was frustrated.

I told him that even if he didn't want to resume his counselling sessions or talk about medicine, I hoped he was at least still journalling.

"No, I'm not. I don't journal anymore," he said.

"Well, why not?" I asked, immediately disappointed. "It's supposed to be healthy and therapeutic to write out your feelings."

"No," he countered. "Writing is not for everyone. It's not for me."

"What do you mean?" I asked. "Why not?"

"I don't like writing out my thoughts," he said with his head down, looking at the kitchen table. "It scares me."

My heart stopped. Or so it felt.

"What do you mean it scares you?" I asked, almost afraid to hear the answer.

He was quiet.

"Jamal, do you still think about hurting yourself?"

"Ya. Sometimes," he said, without making eye contact. "I know I won't do it. But it just pops in my head. I don't know why. I don't want to think about it, so I just sleep. All I want is to be happy. What's so damn hard about that?" he asked as he became visibly upset and irritated.

I sat down beside him and talked for a moment about the importance of getting help. Once again, I assured him that he wasn't alone. I told him how important he was to our family and how much we loved him and were there to support him every step of the way.

My heart hurt.

He insisted he wasn't going to do anything to hurt himself and that he was just having random thoughts.

He insisted he didn't want to go back to counselling.

He insisted he didn't need medication.

He insisted he was done journalling about his feelings.

What was I supposed to do? He was twenty-one years old and I couldn't force him to do anything he didn't want to.

Going to bed that night, I could not ease my mind enough to actually fall into a good sleep.

I tossed and turned until my alarm sounded. Time for work.

Chapter 15

The weeks passed as Jamal's mood seemed to stay flat-lined. He was irritable and would isolate himself in his room most of the time.

We'd never allowed television in our kids' rooms from the beginning, and still at Jamal's age, he didn't have one. But he did have his laptop and a computer monitor to play his video games on. Funny thing is, Jamal was never a huge gamer. He would play at times but really was never the type of kid to sit in his room every day, gaming for hours. Now it seemed that when he was tired of lying in bed and sleeping all day, he would game. I guess it gave him something different to focus on and redirect his thoughts.

Jamal had, and continues to have, an amazing small group of friends.

They are great guys who he grew up with and who he has a real brotherhood with.

During this time when he was in such a deep slump, his friends would often stop by and sit in his room with him just chatting. I was happy when they stopped in because

I knew he wasn't making any effort to go out and do things with them.

Every time they would visit, I would see a new positive phrase written on the whiteboard that he had screwed onto his wall. I had bought it for him at our last house to be used somewhat as a vision board. I felt that if he wrote things down, whether a To Do list or goal setting, it would help with his anxiety and daily focus points. I was happy to see that he was using it.

His friends would write things like, "Positive thoughts create a positive day." Or, "Stay focused and just do it!" Their notes always made me smile.

And he always made lists of things he needed to get done. It made me feel good knowing there were conversations around his feelings with his close friends and that he was planning or at least intending to do things.

Secretly, it gave me a little sense of security that he was planning to be around to get those things done.

A month or so before Christmas, my mom arrived from the city for a visit. She would be staying for one week.

As she settled in, Jamal emerged from his room in the basement to say hi to Grandma.

She was always happy to see him, especially since he was the only grandson still living with us at home. After a big Grandma-hug and some catching up, he asked when dinner would be ready. I was actually surprised to hear him ask, since he barely had an appetite.

"Another thirty minutes or so," I answered.

"Okay, call me when it's ready," he said. Then he disappeared into his room in the basement.

After he was completely out of earshot, my mom looked at me with panic and worry in her eyes.

"He doesn't look good. He is so thin! My goodness, he's lost so much weight.

And I can just look at him and see that he is not happy. He's not well," she said.

"Has he been to the doctor lately?"

"Nope," I said. "He doesn't want to."

"But he's not well. I can just look at him and see that," she repeated, as though I hadn't heard her the first time.

"I know, Mom. I know. But I can't force him to go to the doctor. And besides, our doctor won't do anything for him anyway, except say that he's going through a phase of not eating. I'm done talking to our doctor about his depression. He doesn't need our family doctor; he needs to reconnect with his counsellor. But he doesn't want to. He says he's doing his own depression management by reading about the different types of depression in an effort to try and understand it somewhat," I explained.

"He's been meditating daily and he tries to work out at least a few times a week. I don't know, Mom. I really just don't know what else to do."

I felt my eyes beginning to tear up.

"All I can do is watch him closely, monitor his behaviour, and keep talking to him. There's nothing else I can do. I honestly barely even sleep anymore." I just felt trained.

She looked at me and simply shook her head, as if to say, "There has to be something more we can do."

But instead her words were, "I know it's hard. I know. I can only imagine."

Jamal's depression either had me feeling helpless or annoyed. It just depended on his mood and what scenarios were being played out at any given time. After this short conversation with my mom, my mood was the feeling of helplessness.

Dinner was ready. I had been sure to make something I knew Jamal would like: mashed potatoes with roast beef and gravy to die for.

I called Jamal upstairs, excited to see him eat. I yelled, "Dinner!"

He came back upstairs, walked into the kitchen, opened the lid to the beef, looked at it, took a deep breath of the aroma, and then placed the lid back on. He said, "Looks good. I'm not hungry yet though. I'll eat a little later."

Disappointed, I knew later would mean, not today.

"What do you mean?" I asked, annoyed. "What have you eaten today besides nothing?"

"I had two boiled eggs today. I'm just not hungry, Mom," he said as he started walking back down to the basement. "I'll come up and eat later."

"You're gonna melt away to nothing, Jamal," I shouted after him. "It's not healthy to not eat. Look at how much weight you've lost."

"I'm fine, Mom. I'll eat later. It's not a big deal," he said.

But it was. It was a huge deal.

I didn't see him back in the kitchen that night.

Chapter 16

I found myself in a constant battle in my own head where Jamal's depression was concerned. As a mom, I was very aware of how real it was because I was the one home most of the time to see him, spend time with him, notice the differences in his mood and behaviour, and get a real sense of how things were unfolding.

I was the one he talked to. He would send a text message telling me what a crappy day he was having, or on good days he would tell me about something nice or exciting that had happened to change his mood.

Then there was my husband's perception of why Jamal was struggling and not feeling "on par."

He honestly agreed with our doctor that Jamal was just going through a phase.

He felt Jamal didn't know what he wanted to do career-wise while seeing his friends make decisions to go away to school, do apprenticeships, or get into a line of work they really enjoyed. He felt that because of this, Jamal was feeling lost and overwhelmed.

As parents we do whatever we can to protect our children. We try our best to set them up for success to make their lives less painful, less stressful, less disappointing, less of anything that isn't deemed successful or good. But sometimes, there are things that happen outside of our control. I knew the severity of Jamal's feelings and I understood that his depression was real. It wasn't a phase, or an upset. It was something that he desperately hated. He wished he could find a way to make it stop.

I understood it. But I wasn't going to force this understanding onto my husband or anyone else. His depression was something that was just outside of our control. No matter how much we wanted to change it, we couldn't.

I started thinking that maybe his depression stemmed from a combination of a lot of things.

Maybe losing his uncle at a young age and not being able to talk about it had impacted him more than we knew.

Maybe being a part of a rep hockey team had been more exciting, demanding, and mentally challenging than he would ever admit to us.

Maybe being a teenager and living up to expectations set by friends and family, along with his own, caused a lack of confidence.

Maybe broken relationships along the way caused doubt and disappointment.

Maybe having scoliosis and going through major back surgery just before his senior year of football was devastating enough to make him want to just give up on everything.

Maybe writing the military tests and not being successful for something he felt (at the time) so passionately about had taken the wind right out of whatever sail he had left.

Maybe feeling he didn't have a sense of direction or purpose after graduating high school had left him confused and anxious.

Maybe all the negative self-talk and shaken confidence did just that — shook him — to the point where he couldn't help himself anymore.

So many "maybes" filled my mind. I searched desperately for a reason that would make sense to me, a reason that would validate my "why". To me, the "why" was important, because if we found out why, there could be a way to fix it.

I didn't have the answers. I was just a mother with a child who was struggling every day with mental health.

I wish we could have requested an X-ray of his head that would give us a solid image or reason for why he felt the way he did. I wish it would have told us what magic pill we needed to fix it. But we couldn't.

That's not the way mental illness works.

Looking back, one of the things I've realized is that he was so good at pretending everything was okay.

He learned to say and do the things he needed to in order to slip under the radar of our questions and harassing comments about his feelings and behaviour.

I found an online article that talked about "Perfectly Hidden Depression." (PHD)

The article spoke about people who suffer in silence. They learn how to act, how to speak, and how to behave as if their life was great, nothing too crazy or out of control that they couldn't handle.

These people slide under the radar from friends and loved ones suspecting that anything may be wrong. They pretend that everything in their lives is great. Often times, they are the funny ones, the life of the party, the first one to extend a helping hand or give advice to others having a hard time in their own lives. They are popular and have many people who would describe them as giving, happy-go-lucky, friendly, and always ready to help... But these people who suffer from PHD unfortunately are the same people who are much more likely to take their own lives suddenly and quietly by suicide.

The article hit me hard.

It manifested so many emotions in me. I felt sick because I knew that for the longest time, this was my son. Throughout his teenage years, he was a master of hiding the pain and suffering he was going through.

It was only at nineteen, when he shared his experiences and feelings with his then girlfriend, Carrie, that we became shockingly aware of this illness.

If he had never shared this, I might not have my son here today.

I felt nauseous, scared, and grateful all at the same time.

Looking back, I almost feel that if Jamal were diagnosed with bipolar, I would believe it. Some days, he was happy and so bubbly. He was a ball of excited energy.

He had so much energy and passion about an idea or a new opportunity that he would work at it all day and night if he needed to. Then, it would seem like days later, he would crash.

He was miserable and genuinely unhappy, wanting nothing to do with anyone or anything.

He would turn away and ignore his friends. He would make plans to meet up with them, and then cancel at the last minute and do nothing but lay in bed or on the couch in the basement watching television.

I thought to myself, "Was the happy and bubbly attitude just a facade to mask the real sadness and pain he was truly feeling?"

I don't know. I'm not an expert. But I do know this illness is extremely complicated.

I found myself digging through memories in my brain to find reasons. I would recall times of frustration with Jamal. I remembered the day, as a teen, when he told off his boss at the fast food restaurant. She said something to him in a tone that made him feel disrespected. He told her exactly how he felt about that, in many descriptive words, and walked out.

I remember him coming home and telling me all about it and how upset he was.

Then he flat-out refused to apply for any other job. He was done and wanted no part of it.

I don't remember at the time why I seemed to be okay with that decision, but I was. Looking back, I think had I forced him to go back to work, it could have been his breaking point.

This subject was so taboo years ago, especially within minority communities.

I can tell you that within the Caribbean community, when someone acted "a little off",

it was either laughed at, ignored, or the person was outcast and deemed crazy.

Unless they were completely out of control and deemed a danger to themselves or others, nothing was done. There was no suggestion of help. No support system. The person was just expected to get over it.

Growing up in a strong Jamaican household, there was no special attention given to any of us when we were sad or disappointed. Life happened. Disappointments happened. But you showed strength by "getting over it." And moving on.

Some may feel that this type of upbringing was too harsh. Looking back, I can say that yes, at times it was. But it taught me strength and the ability to cope with failures. More importantly, it taught me to **expect** failures in life.

I've had many discussions with some of my closest Caribbean friends and family, and we agree that we've all had very similar upbringings. Our upbringings have led to both positive and negative reflections of how they have impacted our lives as adults and what they have taught us.

I learned all that glitters is not gold. And that life would unexpectedly kick me in the belly and knock the wind right out of me.

But it was up to me to choose to get back up, because if I didn't, I would be stepped on as others kept on moving.

My upbringing gave me coping skills that taught me how to hide my pain, ignore the feelings of defeat and disappointment, and shake it off.

But when I think about it, I also realize that I became conditioned to expect disappointment.

I became conditioned to dismiss my feelings and other people's feelings of defeat and disappointment. And so over time, one can begin to lose themselves and the ability to feel, or to truly cope with the emotions they experience, which ironically, can cause a buildup of all kinds of unhealthy behaviours, beliefs, and even mental health issues... (But that's a whole other book.)

My point is, that mental health is indeed complicated.

It's not black or white. And it's hard for those who are struggling daily to cope.

It is also difficult for those supporting the ones who are struggling.

There is no magic pill. No magic potion.

Dismissing it or wishing it away will not make it disappear.

We all have to try, because by trying, we are providing hope and possibility.

Jamal continued to have good days and bad days. But the one thing I noticed was his excitement for his course at school.

At twenty-two, he had enrolled in psychology at our local college and was thoroughly enjoying the course. He studied several topics dealing with mental health and what caused people to feel and behave the way they did. It almost seemed therapeutic for him. He would spend hours in his room completing his assignments. He focused hard and met deadlines. After completing the semester, he successfully wrote his exams and finished with a ninety-two per cent GPA!

Mid-spring, he began reconnecting with an old girlfriend he had known in grade nine.

This was surprising to me, because he had been adamantly single for the past year and a half and was reluctant to get involved with anyone while he focused on himself. But I had started to see a happier, more content Jamal and was welcoming of the positive change.

He talked more, went out more with friends, and seemed to be trying to cope by talking out his feelings more openly with me.

He definitely still had cloudy days, but I saw progress and I was excited.

More and more, I could see the relationship with his girlfriend taking form and becoming serious.

They spent a lot of time together and reconnected now on a more mature level, which was good to witness!

She had recently completed four years of university and was taking a break before deciding what path she wanted to take in her career. My son had found his passion in school for psychology.

They had a lot in common and seemed to balance each other.

Where she struggled with dealing with confrontation and a little anxiety at work or between family and friends, Jamal showed her coping skills.

When he was down and having a bad day, she would allow him time to deal with his emotions and feelings and would give him the space he needed before talking it through.

They both enjoyed the outdoors and getting out to take part in social community events.

It was nice to see and I enjoyed being able to watch the growth of a healthy relationship.

Early that fall, Jamal came into the kitchen as I stood making dinner and said he needed to talk to me and his dad. But since his dad always worked late, he would talk to me first.

He told me that his girlfriend had been offered a job opportunity in a different province with the company she worked for. They were opening a new and larger location and had offered her the opportunity to move there, help with the hiring process, set up, and open the location as Assistant

Supervisor. It was a great opportunity in a beautiful province in eastern Canada where she had always dreamed of living. It was something she didn't want to pass up, and in fact, she had already accepted.

He told me he had taken a few days to think about it and decided that he didn't want a long-distance relationship. Instead, he had researched the university there and was elated to see his course was offered. He assured me that he had researched the school's standings within the region and was excited to see they were highly recommended. Though a small school, it was a well-recognized facility.

He even did his homework to see the number of visible minorities within the city and to check how he would fit into the community, as well as cost of school and living expenses.

Simply put, he had already made up his mind that he would be moving out of the province before Christmas to embark on a new and exciting journey.

My immediate reaction was surprise, then sadness, then worry, then excitement.

All in that very order.

"Mom, I gotta try new things. I really think I need a change," he said, eyes wide open.

"Before this, I was even thinking of applying to go teach English overseas somewhere. I really want to do this," he said with a smile so wide I couldn't help but smile myself.

"Jamal, I don't know. Are you sure about this?" I asked slowly, looking him directly in his eyes.

"Yeeessss!" he said. "I am so sure! This is what I want. It's scary but so exciting at the same time!" He searched my face for approval.

My heart was full. I could see that he really was excited and had done his homework to come prepared with answers to all of my anticipated questions.

"Okay," I said. "If this is what you want, I'm happy for you. It's a chance of a lifetime that you would never have taken if this opportunity didn't present itself, so I say go for it!"

"Yes Mom!" he said, pumping his fist. "I'm so pumped!" I gave him a hug and he disappeared back into his room to call his girlfriend.

I spent the next few hours trying to assure myself this was a good thing and that it would be good for him to be on his own, learn about life, and be an independent adult living in his own space. I tried to convince myself that he was twenty-two years old and would grow immensely from this experience.

I wasn't concerned about him being successful at school, or finding a job, or the relationship with his girlfriend. My first and primary concern was focused solely on his mental health.

I had been his biggest support, his one consistent. I was the one who understood him. I knew when he was having a bad day and how to try and make it better by doing the little things. Buying him his favourite candy treats, picking up a card and writing words of encouragement, bringing home the scented candles he loved to burn, or making his favourite meal from childhood for dinner or something specific he had asked for.

Regardless, I knew how to take care of him. He needed me and I wasn't sure that leaving home would change that.

But as the days passed and I pondered, I quickly realized that he was ready to stand on his own two feet and it was me who wasn't prepared for it to happen.

After telling the rest of the family, I remember my husband and daughter poking fun at me by saying, "Oh your favourite son is leaving home. What are you gonna do? You're going to cry your eyes out." I completely dismissed their silliness.

All this time, I had considered myself his guardian, his crutch. But instead, he had become my crutch. He didn't need protecting anymore. He had grown wings and was ready to take a risk at living his life with no guarantees that things would work out. He was willing to try, which is something that he had not dared to even consider before. In my realization, I moved from sad and concerned to proud and hopeful.

He was setting himself up with the best chance for success and was willing to try. That's all I could have asked for and it was good enough for me.

Jamal's girlfriend moved out of the province a few weeks before he did. She needed to be there to get started at work. There was lots to do. So, for the first three weeks, she was at the new apartment alone, working long hours daily.

On the weekend before Christmas we held a special early Christmas dinner for two reasons:

1. My husband and I had booked our vacation to visit with family in the Caribbean and would be flying out Christmas Eve.
2. Jamal was leaving to join his girlfriend four days before Christmas.

Christmas was important to us and we wanted to make sure our family had a special Christmas celebration. And we did. We had a lovely dinner with the whole family.

Three days later, I tried to mentally prepare myself for driving Jamal to the airport.

I lay awake that night with racing thoughts and serious anxiety.

My chest hurt and I felt as though I was having a panic attack. I jumped out of bed and went to the kitchen for a cold glass of water. I stood there in the dark, silently, holding my glass as tears streamed down my face. After about ten minutes, I pulled myself together, headed back upstairs to my room, and quietly slid into my en-suite bathroom. I blew my nose, washed my face with cold water, gently slid back into bed, and melted into my husband. I was fine. It was all going to be fine.

I managed to sleep well that night.

The next day was Jamal's moving day. I woke up feeling excited for him. I knew he must be anxious, so the last thing he needed was to see me emotional or upset.

I held it together. His flight wasn't until later that night. For the entire day, he wrapped up loose ends and finished his last-minute packing. When it was time to leave for the airport, he said his goodbyes to his sister, older brother, and grandparents. He called his dad and then younger brother to say his goodbyes from the car as we headed to the airport.

At the airport, I parked the car and walked him into the departure terminal. As we got him checked in and organized, my anxiety slowly left me. I walked him to the entry doors, which was as far as I could go. I hugged him tight and told him I loved him and to text me as soon as he landed. His girlfriend would be there to pick up him up. He seemed calm but excited.

I watched him walk through the doors and was glad the large glass windows allowed me to see inside until he was cleared through customs. I watched him the entire time. After he retrieved his belongings from the X-ray belt, he lastly put on his backpack and waved to me with a smile. Then he disappeared through the large frosted doors. He was now on his way, flying solo.

Chapter 17

As the weeks past, I became more at ease. Jamal was only a two-hour flight away, and we talked on a daily basis. He was so proud of their apartment. He would walk me through it by video on his phone, showing me the rooms and how they had decorated. It was always clean as a whistle with everything in its place. He would show me the awesome dinners that he cooked. He had found a real interest in experimenting in the kitchen, which he never did at home with us. His girlfriend was impressed with his skills and effort and I couldn't be happier to see this side of my son. He often expressed how excited he was to explore the city. They loved the outdoors and seemed genuinely happy.

Jamal found a job almost immediately, which was great. He spoke about how well he was treated by the people he worked with. He had a full-time day job and was starting to look for a part-time job as well.

But as the weeks and months rolled on, I could hear a change in Jamal's voice.

He didn't seem excited anymore. Oftentimes when I asked him why he sounded down, he would say he was just tired. But I knew better.

A mother's intuition is never wrong. After a few conversations, he started to share with me that he and his girlfriend were having problems. Her stress level was high with work and it seemed that moving halfway across the country had become a bigger stressor for her than she had originally thought. It was causing her anxiety which seemed to worsen a little each day.

I would often tell him to just be patient. I tried to reassure him that things would settle down and everything would be fine. Some conversations were great and I could tell that he was okay. But other times I could hear the sadness and frustration in his voice. He felt he was trying so hard but all they seemed to do was argue over stupid things, all because she was overwhelmed and over sensitive.

During this time, my mother-in-law became gravely ill. She was hospitalized and then sent home to be as comfortable as possible. We knew we had limited time left with her.

On the morning she passed away, we contacted all the children to let them know and booked Jamal on a next-day flight back home.

My husband picked him up from the airport. When he walked into the house, I was so excited to see him. But I couldn't believe how thin he was. I could immediately see the weight loss.

"You've lost weight," I said.

"Ya, I know," he said quietly. That was the end of that conversation.

The funeral services were arranged quickly, just the way my mother-in-law had requested.

It was a wonderful tribute to her life, and as a family, we said our final goodbyes.

Through it all, the children held up as best as they could have.

During his short visit, Jamal reconnected with his close friends. It was nice to see. And a few days later, I drove him back to the airport. As we drove, I talked about the importance of being happy and not allowing anything or anyone to get in the way of that. I assured him that I was always just a phone call away and that **he** was in charge of his life and how he wanted to live it. He assured me that everything would be okay and all in all, he was really enjoying the experience of being in such a different environment. He was excited about enrolling in school in the fall. He looked forward to the future. I was happy to hear his optimism and sent him on his way with a big hug.

Spring arrived and the weather was warm and welcomed. Jamal was looking forward to getting out to find trails and different places to explore. But each time we spoke, his mood was like a roller coaster. I could tell that he was once again struggling mentally.

The beginning of April, Jamal called me and told me that he and his girlfriend had made a mutual decision to end their relationship. And, after only five months, they had both decided they were moving back home.

I was happy to hear the news.

They agreed on a timeline of three months. It was a difficult but mature decision, and I was proud of him. They obviously still cared about each other and wanted an amicable split.

A few weeks later as I sat working in my home office, I received a call from him. He sounded very sad. His words were slow as though it was draining what little energy he had left. As we talked, I asked him why he wasn't at work. He paused, and then said, "All I do is lay in bed. I can't eat, I can't sleep, and I'm having bad thoughts again. I just don't want to be here anymore."

Immediately, my mind started racing with the worst thoughts possible. These were the words I never wanted to hear — ever again.

When he said, "I just don't want to be here anymore," he wasn't talking about living away from home. He was talking about living.

I went into panic/recovery mode.

Without hesitation, I told him he was coming home immediately. I told him that we would book a flight for him and I didn't care what the plan was for the next coming weeks that they had agreed to. I wanted him home **now**.

We would just have to work out the details of a full move later. I told him to pack his suitcase with all his belongings and we would send the flight information to him via email as soon as we confirmed things.

Before hanging up, I made him promise me that he wouldn't do anything to harm himself. He promised.

Then, I immediately sent a text message to my daughter, frantically explaining the conversation I just had with her brother. As tears streamed down my face, I could feel my heart beating out of my chest. She called me right away. "He has to come home now," she said, her voice filled with concern.

"Yes, he is," I said. "I told him that."

Without hesitation, she said, "I'll pay for his flight. Just book it."

We booked him on a flight home for the following day.

I called my husband at work and explained the situation. I told him we had booked Jamal's flight home. He agreed that we needed to get him home right away. Things had just spun out of control and he needed to be back at home in a supportive environment.

Chapter 18

The following day, as I drove to the airport to pick him up, I was anxious to see him.

I was relieved that he had actually got on the plane. I worried because he felt guilty for leaving his girlfriend alone. But when he texted me from the gate as he sat and waited to board his flight, my mind was at ease. It wasn't what they had agreed on but it was necessary for his own stability.

As I waited anxiously, he emerged through the large double doors and I walked towards my son with arms wide open.

He was so thin. He was six foot one, and the leanest I had ever seen him. His face was drawn, his eyes were tired. I welcomed him back and we headed home.

The next day, we talked about the situation and how he was feeling. He was sad that things hadn't worked out but was glad to be home. He and his now ex-girlfriend continued to text each other. They continued to plan the details of the move and tried to make things as easy as possible.

I could see that he was really trying but I also saw that he was struggling. I realized myself, that I was struggling. I was angry.

I was angry that I sent a happy and healthier minded boy to embark on an exciting journey, and now months later was returned broken.

The weekend was approaching and I was heading to the United States with my girlfriend for the long weekend.

We had planned this trip a few months earlier.

I felt guilty leaving but convinced myself that he was a grown boy and that he would be okay. I was leaving him at home with his dad, sister, and grandfather. He was in good hands.

The night before I left, I wanted to say a proper goodbye, since I would be leaving very early the next morning. I knocked on his bedroom door and heard a very faint answer.

When I turned the knob and opened the door, Jamal was sitting in the dark, with lights off, blinds closed. He was sitting at the edge of his bed with his head in his hands.

I walked over to him and put my hands on his shoulders. "Hey, what's wrong? What's going on?" I asked quietly. No answer. "Jamal, talk to me. What's going on? What are you feeling right now?"

"I feel like a failure," he snapped angrily. "Everything I try fails."

"What do you mean? What are you talking about? That's not true," I said, matter-of-fact.

"Yes, it is," he said. I realized in that moment that he was feeling completely and utterly defeated. It was so apparent that he was devastated things hadn't worked out. He was disappointed with himself, but I also realized he was upset at the thought that he had also disappointed his dad and I.

Switching on his night table lamp, I stood in front of him listing reason after reason why he should be so proud of himself.

He had battled his way back from a horrible depression.

He had enrolled himself in school and completed his semester with honours.

He was a constant counsel for his younger brother any time he was needed.

He had been a beacon of strength to his girlfriend when she was overwhelmed and going through her own struggles.

He was a great friend and a fantastic son.

But in that moment, I realized that when **he** looked at his life, he only saw failure.

It was the furthest thing from the truth. Yes, disappointments happened and "failures" occurred along the way, as they do in everyone's life. He was not immune.

But I explained to him that every disappointment should become a lesson learned.

If we learn from our "failures", it will only strengthen our ability to bear the future stresses in life.

I stood there for what seemed to be a long time, stern in my discussion and strong in my delivery. I needed him to know that he mattered. I needed him to see what I saw:

a strong, determined, and very capable young man with his entire future ahead of him.

He was passionate about his hope to continue studying psychology. He wanted to become a mentor and psychologist to youth and young adults, as well as athletes who played on a national level.

He wanted to use his experiences to help save and change people's lives.

"You have a purpose in this life," I told him. "You have so much to share, and you can make a difference in other people's lives. I love you and believe in you, but you have to believe in yourself."

At that very moment, I physically saw a light bulb go on in his eyes. I knew in that instant, something I said had clicked. He heard me. Instinctively, I knew he heard me and this time it was different.

I hugged him and told him I would be leaving in the morning but to talk to his dad or sister if he felt he needed to. I also reminded him that I was only a phone call away. I encouraged him to get out of his room, be sure to eat, and go for a walk or two.

I barely slept but in the morning, I went on my way.

Final Chapter

As we drove to the United States, my girlfriend and I chatted about Jamal's situation. She has always been my rock. She has a great ear. When we switched off driving and I took the wheel, my cell phone rang. It was Jamal. My girlfriend answered. I heard her ask him how he was feeling and what kind of day he was having. To my surprise, it seemed like it was good news!

She put the phone on speaker so I could talk to him directly.

He sounded amazing! His voice was light and happy. He said he had already eaten both breakfast and lunch. He had mowed the lawn for his dad and was doing good.

I was elated! We talked a little more and I ended our call by saying, "Stay strong and try to keep a positive mindset. I'm so glad you're feeling better and you are up and doing things. Proud of you!"

I was sure the reason he called me was to put my mind at ease and share how much better he was feeling. With that, my mind was clear and my trip was enjoyable.

Over one year has passed. Today, Jamal is doing very well. He is attending university and studying psychology. He completed first year with honors!

His dad and I couldn't be happier.

He is passionate about his future. He has reconnected with his amazing group of friends, and tries every day to live his best life.

He finally made the decision to seek help through an outpatient program at our local hospital and decided to accept medication as part of his treatment plan. He's been officially diagnosed with anxiety and depression.

I've noticed a huge improvement and I feel that we have our son back.

He's committed to his studies and to his future.

I couldn't be happier with his progress and maturity.

I also feel that maturing has helped immensely with his reflections on his life.

I know that as a teen battling anxiety, everything in that moment, no matter how small or fixable, can manifest itself into a massive and sometime catastrophic feeling of helplessness.

Through this sometimes terrifying journey, I have watched him grow and mature into a fine young man. I see how he now analyzes situations in a much healthier way. He uses reasoning and logic to properly assess the true significance, if any, of challenges that arise. As his mom, it's been incredibly rewarding for me to see such growth.

For anyone struggling with mental illness, or supporting a loved one who is, no two journeys are alike.

As a mother, I can only stress that you are not alone.

For myself, I did not seek professional help or support, though I always knew it was available. I think I took this approach because of who I am.

I am a thinker. I tend to research things on my own, talk my feelings and emotions through, and look within myself for opportunities to find healing. I suppose this ability comes from my active practice as a Life Coach. But we all deal with trials and turbulence in many different ways. I could have definitely benefited by seeking out a support group.

For those who feel they need to connect with a supportive community, there are resources and support systems all across the country that are committed to helping you. Please know that you do not have to walk this path in silence.

For parents, family members, and friends who are doing their best to support those struggling with mental illness, please do not give up on them.

On the darkest of days where you feel frustrated and defeated, do not give up.

There is help for you as well.

Resources are available to teach us how to recognize warning signs that we may otherwise dismiss. We can learn how to strategically avoid and handle confrontation, as well as gain positive coping skills.

If we as parents and supporters give up on our loved ones who struggle, then the illness wins.

By committing to learn more about mental health, we will have a better understanding of the behaviours we see and experience.

Mental illness is crippling to some and can be very scary and confusing for those who struggle. But by being involved, we can become an important piece of the puzzle.

Dealing with someone with a mental illness is not easy. Parents who see their child struggling daily, while knowing there is nothing they can do to protect them, may often experience a sense of helplessness. But I have learned that knowledge is power. Becoming involved in the conversation gives me the drive and determination I need to help create better processes and to offer support.

I have accepted this challenge with an open heart and recognize this will be an ongoing battle for my son. But I refuse to stay silent or accept defeat. Today I speak publicly to audiences about mental health. I have founded a nonprofit organization which hosts events to raise funds for our local hospital's Mental Health and Addictions Unit. I host seminars and have formed a support group for those supporting loved ones, young people and adults with mental illness.

My belief is that conversation cultivates awareness, and awareness brings support.

And where there is support, there is hope.

The End

Manufactured by Amazon.ca
Bolton, ON

29602361R00079